Political Stability and Religion: Fundamentalism in Perspective

Martin Fuller

May 1996

Wilton Park Paper 119

Report based on Wilton Park Conference 452: 30 October–3 November 1995 on "Religion and Political Stability: Fundamentalism in Perspective".

London: HMSO   Hobson Library

318402

© Crown copyright 1996
Applications for reproduction should be made to
HMSO's Copyright Unit, St Clements House, 2–16 Colegate,
Norwich NR3 1BQ

ISBN 0 11 701907 0
ISSN 0953 8542

Published by HMSO and available from:
HMSO Publications Centre
(Mail, fax and telephone orders only)
PO Box 276, London SW8 5DT
Telephone orders 0171 873 9090
General enquiries 0171 873 0011
(queuing system in operation for both numbers)
Fax orders 0171 873 8200

HMSO Bookshops
49 High Holborn, London WC1V 6HB
(counter service only)
0171 873 0011 Fax 0171 831 1326
68–69 Bull Street, Birmingham B4 6AD
0121 236 9696 Fax 0121 236 9699
33 Wine Street, Bristol BS1 2BQ
0117 926 4306 Fax 0117 929 4515
9–21 Princess Street, Manchester M60 8AS
0161 834 7201 Fax 0161 833 0634
16 Arthur Street, Belfast BT1 4GD
01232 238451 Fax 01232 235401
71 Lothian Road, Edinburgh EH3 9AZ
0131 479 3141 Fax 0131 479 3142
The HMSO Oriel Bookshop
The Friary, Cardiff CF1 4AA
01222 395548 Fax 01222 384347

HMSO's Accredited Agents
(see Yellow Pages)

and through good booksellers

Contents

		page
1	**Introduction**	1
2	**Religious Ideals and Political Practice**	7
3	**Case Studies: Islam and the Middle East**	8
	Unholy Alliance: Can Muslim and Jewish Religious Extremists Derail the Peace Process?	8
	Islam in Government and in Opposition	13
	Iran	13
	Algeria	15
4	**Case Studies: Asia**	18
	Pakistan: Can a Muslim Society Function in a Secular State?	18
	Hindu Nationalism: Setting the Political Agenda?	20
	Islam in South-East Asia	23
	Could Islamism Provoke Destabilisation in Central Asia?	25
5	**Case Studies: Europe**	29
	Former Yugoslavia: the Role of Religion in the Creation of National Identities and in Promoting War	29
	Roman Catholicism in Poland	31
6	**The Forgotten Fundamentalists: Christians in Africa and Latin America**	33
	Christian Fundamentalism in Southern Africa	33
	Catholicism, Protestantism and Politics in Latin America	36
7	**Conclusions**	39
	List of Participants	41

1 Introduction

Religion remains a major political force at the end of the millenium: yet only a generation ago, religion seemed a clearly waning force in politics. Then, the global conflict of the superpowers was reflected in the contest of their ideologies, of Marxism versus Western democracy. Regionally, local socialisms, often quasi-Marxist, challenged or ousted traditional regimes. Hence in 1960, the eminent historian of the Middle East, the late Albert Hourani, could credibly describe the anti-Western Muslim Brotherhood as "an archaistic movement in a society which had already changed" – even when it was founded, in 1928.[1]

The analysts of the 1960s could not have foreseen the collapse of Soviet communism and the end of the super-power conflict, with its profound implications for the regional clients of the former Soviet Union. Many local socialisms and ideologies have disappeared, others survive only in name. Internationally, such once formidable political phenomena as the Non-Aligned Movement have also faded. Regionally and internationally, the secular challenge to Western ideas has largely disappeared, leaving the field in much of the world to religion. Even where there is no challenge to the West, religion frequently provides the means to assert national or ethnic identity. With its resurgence as a political force, much of the world's political landscape at the end of the 20th century resembles more that at the close of the 19th, than that of the more secular mid-20th century.

General academic opinion holds that 'fundamentalism' is an unsatisfactory term, but there seems no alternative, particularly given the widespread media usage. Modern usage dates from the US Protestant 'Creationists', who opposed Darwin's Theory of Evolution, but a 'fundamentalist' can simply be one who follows the basic tenets of his or her religion literally, without political connotations. However, in the West it has become a largely

---

[1] A.H. Hourani, preface to J.M. Ahmed, *The Intellectual Origins of Egyptian Nationalism*, Royal Institute of International Affairs/OUP, London, 1960.

political and pejorative term: 'fundamentalism' equals extremism and is bad, while 'moderation' is good. This is especially true of 'Islamic fundamentalism', frequently a shopping list of its opponents' fears. In the US, Professor Sam Huntington has characterised militant Islam as the foe of Western democracy, while former NATO Secretary-General Willy Claes also saw it as the West's political enemy. Such views essentially see militant Islam as a threat to replace Soviet Communism. Other Western opinions, official and non-official, consider it a threat to economic interests and to human rights, while in the Middle East, governments of nations such as Egypt and Algeria, themselves Muslim, have reason to see it as a threat to their regimes.

More analytical and perhaps less alarmist opinions, however, see 'fundamentalism' and the upsurge of religious consciousness generally as reactive, a response to pressures. These include economic deprivation, the failure of secular political doctrines to deliver improvements in living conditions, Western and modernising influences, nationalist pressures and external threats. Add to these widely differing regional conditions and perceptions and it is obvious that there are many fundamentalisms, a series of phenomena which defy any neat collective definition.

The economic causes are perhaps the most easily understood. 'Fundamentalism' is conspicuously a phenomenon of developing and underdeveloped countries, where lack of resources is often accompanied by high population growth, resulting in a disproportionately young population with few prospects of employment. Traditional parties and philosophies such as Marxism are perceived to have failed. Sometimes, governments face calls from international lending institutions for financial discipline: the resulting hardships bear hardest on ordinary people, fuelling resentment against both their own governments and the West. Much needed expertise is often lost when the most able and educated emigrate, but many migrants to the West then become impoverished minorities, again hardest-hit by unemployment. With confidence in the state lost, the alternatives offered by religious groups are attractive, the more so when they provide a practical, as well as a moral, example. Hamas, notorious for its suicide bomber attacks on Israeli buses, first won popular support in Gaza for its mosque-based social welfare programmes. Beneficiaries may be receptive to its claims that 'Islam is the answer', but religious movements cannot substitute for the resources of a state. Islamic groups are not pharmacies dispensing prescriptive remedies, for example, no-one has devised an 'Islamic' solution to the Cairo housing problem. Beyond the Middle East, India's Bharatiya Janata Party (BJP) effectively exploits economic deprivation in pursuit of nationalist aims. But south-east Asia is the exception which proves the rule. Economies there are prospering (even Indonesia has checked its population growth and fed its people for 30 years) and there is little threat from 'fundamentalist' movements.

Identity and nationalism are closely associated with religion as a force in politics. Many peoples realise instinctively that religion preserves collective identity, while religious leaders know that their influence depends on public support. So do secular nationalist leaders, who often court religious support to legitimise their power, but whose secular attitudes sometimes make for an uneasy relationship. Not all have the panache of David Ben-Gurion, Israel's first Prime Minister, of whom a Jewish commentator wrote: "Jews have always made impossible demands upon their leaders and have looked not only for competence and integrity but a hint of divine approval. Ben-Gurion was one such figure and, although he did not believe in God himself, he somehow gave the impression that God believed in him".[2] Nationalism is at its strongest when drawing on religious bases, but religion can sanction its most negative aspects, reinforcing divisions of 'us and them', witness Protestants and Catholics in Northern Ireland and Hindus and Muslims in Pakistan. In the latter case, Muslim religious extremists have capitalised on the political overtures of successive governments. In Algeria, nationalists mobilised religious support against France, but when the French left, established a secular regime.

---

[2] Chaim Bermant, *The Observer*, 4 September, 1983.

Now, Algerian religious extremists threaten the unity of the state. The Arab-Israel Dispute is a conflict of nationalisms: on both sides the extremists are inspired by religion. In the former Yugoslavia, opposing nationalists exploit religion to rally popular support. In Central Asia, post-Soviet leaderships have sought legitimacy through Islam, but their opponents too now include Islam in their political platforms. The Catholic Church in Poland, long the focus for national opposition to Communism and an expression of Polish identity, is itself now a cause of dispute among Poles debating the nature of their state. But south-east Asia again provides an exception: only in Malaysia, where the population is almost half Chinese, is Islam used to assert a national Malay character.

Science and modernity challenge all religions, via such contemporary issues as genetic engineering. Science brings benefits to all, but may conflict with individual belief, a conflict which will become more widespread as information technology becomes ever more global. Many non-Westerners see such globalisation and the media as undermining families, breaking up societies and encouraging turmoil. Western debate, liberal, secular, even cynical, is alien to them. Holding fast to values they believe to be superior to those of the West, they fear rapid change and turn to religion, which represents security and stability, their map to Paradise. Hence today's revivalism is in large part a search for stability, certainty and identity in a world of uncertainty, a phenomenon not restricted to poorer countries.

Here lies a major cause of friction with the West and of division between Christianity and other faiths, for modernity and science are essentially Western creations. Religion and Western influence (Christian and post-Christian) have been in conflict over much of the world, but the conflict has been particularly acute for Middle Eastern Muslims and Jews, owing to their involvement in or proximity to Europe. They have been obliged to play political roles, while the ambitions of their more religious members for states defined by Islam and Judaism owe much to reaction against Western influence. The Zionists sought a homeland refuge from their tragedies in Europe, while the Muslims fought to end colonialism. For them, Western modernity is hostile and invasive.

Christian historical experience has not been comparably 'political'. Christ taught that his kingdom is not of this world and the early Christians tried to avoid involvement in the politics of the Roman Empire. Today, Christians do challenge the secular order, but also compromise with it. Three examples emphasise the centrality of schools and education to arguments over the role of religion in society: headscarves for Muslim schoolgirls in Europe, Crucifixes in German classrooms and prayers in US schools. Despite their often vigorous opposition, for Western Christians modernising influences have not come from outside, as invaders to be resisted. The Renaissance, the Industrial Revolution and the rise of Science are Western cultural phenomena, to which Christianity has eventually adjusted, albeit divided by its own revolutionary convulsion, the Reformation. Those who claim literal truth for Scripture against Science, such as the Creationist opponents of Darwinism, remain an isolated minority. By contrast, for all Muslims the Qur'an is the literal Word of God, from which the Sharia (Islamic Law) and Islamic practice derive, providing comprehensive instructions on, for example, punishments, marriage laws, dress, taxes and relations between religious and political authority. Here Islam is less akin to Christianity, with its European division of religion and politics, than to Judaism, which shares a tradition of a community governed by religion and, like Islam, stresses the importance of religious law. Hence the importance to both of religious scholars, rather than a priesthood.

Such differences of belief and experience lead to widely differing religious concepts, including 'fundamentalism'. But all 'fundamentalists', of whatever faith, are selective in their attitudes to modernity. The Jewish 'Haredim', fighting against 'secular modernity', still want modern technological benefits, as do other 'fundamentalists' – especially information technology. In India, the BJP denounces such ostentatious symbols of Western modernity as Kentucky Fried Chicken restaurants but employs modern means to advance its cause, while in Latin America the

Pentecostalists, now eroding the heartlands of Roman Catholicism exploit technology and modern business methods. Selectivity extends to scriptures. For example, in Israel, the pious 'Haredim' and, in the Occupied Territories, the 'Gush Emunim' (Block of the Faithful), a Jewish settlers' movement, are both 'fundamentalist'. Both cite the same texts, but the former prepare for the Messiah by scrupulously observing Jewish law, the latter by occupying land. Muslim 'fundamentalists' look back to real or presumed, idealised pasts, to actual or imagined circumstances, choosing whatever supports the religious frameworks. Such selection is inevitable: how else could they attempt to apply the experience of sixth-century Mecca to the modern world? In general, 'fundamentalists' reject modernity only when modernity itself rejects their religious tenets.

A further distinction between religious and secular political philosophies overlaps issues of identity, modernity and reassurance. Religion answers the great, existential, 'why' questions of life, death, pain and suffering, which affect every individual but to which evolutionary Western philosophies respond with little more than 'impatient silence'. Secular Western thought is more concerned with the question 'how', the explanation of observable phenomena. Indian nationalist thinkers saw the two as complementary, the West having industry, technology and models for modern state government, the East supplying spiritual qualities. But the fiercely-held, literal beliefs of most 'fundamentalists' militate against synthesis or accommodation. This explains, perhaps, why the educated leaders of militant Islamic movements are, paradoxically, almost invariably scientific and technical graduates but rarely of the humanities. *Prima facie*, a scientific education ought to lead them away from 'fundamentalism', yet they have an unshakeable prior commitment to narrow religious belief. The humanities involve free discussion of a whole world view, but 'fundamentalists' require a leap of faith *before* entering any religious/philosophical debate. Adding a technical, even Western, education which answers some of the 'how' questions presents few problems to those confident that they have the only answer to the question 'why'.

2 Religious Ideals and Political Practice

True faith can be seen as a beneficial influence on political issues. In the Islamic world view, everything must be 'informed' by religion. Christians should be 'in the world if not of it'. They were called to work for truth, justice, good relations between all peoples and the right to fullness of life for all. Christians should challenge exclusive policies and structures, as they had in the case of South African apartheid. Society should be inclusive, although this carried dangers of 'us and them' attitudes and, worst, of fanaticism. Even elections had their risks: voters could be cajoled to 'vote Christian', whereupon those elected would act to exclude dissidents. Action should be governed by Christian love, tolerance and respect for others' humanity: Christian love and fanaticism, which is vengeful, dehumanised and based on hate, are incompatible. Religion should question, but not seek to impose its views – an ideal of which historically the Church had sometimes fallen sadly short. However, since Vatican II in the 1960s, Roman Catholicism had moved away from a 'mindset of compulsion'. Conversely, politicians should not identify their policies with God's Holy Mandate, for example by advocating 'family values' to support one particular type of family. Politicians and Christians who tried to restrict Christianity to particular issues merited scepticism. True Christians should work for a broad, compassionate framework, not force everyone into a particular mould.

Islam too enjoins respect for the wider community and human differences: there is no compulsion in religion, according to a divine revelation to the Prophet Muhammad. The Prophet established Islam as a political community at Medina, but it was pluralist, embracing Jews and traditional religions, subjecting all to a common law. After the Prophet's death, the contenders for power selected from the religious texts and the guidance of the Sharia lawyers whatever suited their political objectives. True Islam opposes intolerance and absolutism, seeking to persuade, not to coerce. But exploitation by factional politics has often made it seem harsh, intolerant and violent. Some 20th century 'fundamentalists' had rejected political parties in Islam: there could be only the Party of God and that of the devil. Today, Islamic parties played on emotions, rather than offering practical programmes, and emphasised religious practice. However, the Prophet himself had warned against those who put practice before all else.

Tolerance is a crucial determinant in all religious attitudes to politics. Security is important for tolerance: those who feel secure can afford to question attitudes and beliefs. For minorities, tolerance and the liberal conscience of the majority are vital to survival. Through belief or political commitment, religious movements are becoming increasingly intolerant, perhaps reflecting a faltering confidence in Western liberal values. For the West, tolerance encourages politically stable states, which are generally favourable to Western interests. But those opposed to the West, or who see a religious duty to stop others taking the wrong road, for example Iran, may see tolerance as slack, weak, lazy and irresolute. Intolerant religious 'fundamentalism' thus becomes a formidable destabilising political force, particularly when it reflects dissatisfaction at the economic failures of the state.

These factors are obviously crucial to prospects for political pluralism and democracy. Among Islamic opposition groups, even the Muslim Brotherhood now tentatively argues that the Voice of God is heard through the Voice of the People. While any progress towards political democracy would be widely welcomed in the Middle East, there is much concern that Islamic groups, once elected, would never relinquish power. Since 'God cannot lose an election', the fledgling democracy could be only 'One man, one vote – one time'. Yet even Islamists are adopting some Western ideas, however reluctantly, and Muslims generally are trying to adapt to modernity. Islamic thought needs a reformation and must achieve it in a fraction of the time historically taken by Western Christianity. Even in some parts of the West, political pluralism is still a tender plant; in the Muslim world, democracy will grow if not imposed from outside and if it reflects the popular will.

3 Case Studies: Islam and the Middle East

Unholy Alliance: Can Muslim and Jewish Religious Extremists Derail the Peace Process?

The assassination of Israeli Prime Minister Rabin and the attacks by Palestinian Islamic extremists in the following months on Israeli targets, causing much loss of life, underlined the common purpose of Jewish and Arab religious extremists to destroy the peace process. The former, rooted among the settlers of the West Bank and Gaza Strip, oppose an Israeli withdrawal. The latter consider such withdrawal insufficient, with some still hoping for the ultimate recovery of all Palestine.

Competing Arab and Jewish nationalisms long pre-date the establishment of the State of Israel in 1948. Zionist nationalists, fleeing persecution in Europe, came to Palestine. Arab responses, equally nationalist, sought to prevent the takeover of land. Religion was secondary. Prior to the Zionists, the Jews in Palestine were pious hermits, whose ambition was to die in the Holy Land as much as to live there. In 1900, Palestine contained some 30,000 Jews, little affected by either Zionism or the stirrings of Arab nationalism, who lived among Palestine's 350,000 Arabs and spoke Arabic. All changed between 1905 and 1914 when 60,000 very different Jews arrived, mostly of Russian origin, bringing Marxist, socialist and internationalist influences. Theirs was an alien culture: pious Jews and conservative Arabs alike were scandalised by their aggressive sexual equality and communal living. The Zionists' pioneering agricultural programme reinforced Arab perceptions of Jewish separatism and hunger for land. It brought Arab Muslims and Christians together in efforts to counter Jewish economic and political enterprise.

Religion remained subsidiary to the political causes of the conflict. Riots in 1921 were triggered by a Jewish May Day demonstration in Tel Aviv against Britain, the Mandatory power. In the 1929 riots, religion was exploited for political effect and religious feelings deliberately inflamed. More than 130 Jews were killed. The riots started with a trivial incident at Jerusalem involving seating at the Western or Wailing Wall, part of a site holy to both Arabs and Jews. On the Arab side, the Mufti of Jerusalem, Haj Amin el-Husseini, fomented religious discontent to outmanoeuvre his political Arab rivals. On the Jewish side, it was not the pious but the militant extremist Zionist Vladimir Jabotinsky who inflamed Jewish feeling, boasting 'the wall is ours'.

Between the 1930s and the 1960s, the religious card remained in the background. Nationalist, anti-imperialist and European conflicts took precedence. Now it again plays a part, on both sides. Paradoxically, while the modern world is characterised by scientific progress, it is also marked by false messianism and doomsday soothsaying. The extension of Israeli-held territory in the 1967 war encouraged 'heavy messianism': God's Covenant was apparently fulfilled by the conquests and the pioneers settled the old Biblical place names, while even for secular Israelis, the conquered land provided a security buffer. From some 10,000 mostly religious settlers on the West Bank in 1978, the total has grown to today's 100,000 plus, largely due to financial inducements by Menachem Begin's Likud government aimed at pragmatic settlers attracted by a better lifestyle rather than religion.

Modern Arab Palestinian religious resistance originates from the founding, in Egypt in 1928, of the Muslim Brotherhood. In 1988, during the Palestinian uprising or intifada, Hamas emerged from the Muslim Brotherhood which, under popular pressure for greater militancy, could thus safeguard its political position, by disowning Hamas if it failed. Persistent, if unsubstantiated, reports from both Arab and Israeli sources, hold that Israel initially encouraged Hamas as a counterweight to the Palestine Liberation Organisation (PLO), later to regret this divide-and-rule policy.

Hamas won considerable popular support, especially in Gaza. Its militancy in the intifada was complemented by mosque-based social and charitable work. Following the February 1994 Hebron massacre by the Jewish settler Baruch Goldstein of 29 Muslim worshippers at the Ibrahimi mosque, Hamas promised five retaliatory attacks. These were carried out to deadly effect by suicide bombers, young men inspired to sacrifice their lives by Islam and the promise of heavenly rewards. Hamas became second only to the PLO as a political force and, after the Oslo accords, its main political opposition. Its military wing, named after Izz ad-Din Qassam, a militant Palestinian Islamic leader shot dead by British security forces in the 1930s, remains underground, operating independently of the political leadership. Hamas is also present in neighbouring Arab states, particularly Jordan. Palestine Islamic Jihad (PIJ), a much smaller offshoot of Hamas, performs no social work, but is dedicated solely to armed struggle. PIJ is financed mainly by Iran. Hamas was initially funded by private contributions from Saudi Arabia and the Gulf states, although these are now believed to be much reduced. Recently, the Israeli government has claimed that Britain is the 'focal point' for Hamas fundraising, a claim denied by the British government, although known Hamas members are resident in the UK.

Hamas has traditionally called for the liberation of all Palestine and considers agreement with Israel as humiliation. But between 1993 and 1995, the prospect of participation in elections for a Palestinian autonomous authority exposed some strains in the leadership: if it refused to participate, Arafat would dominate the elected assembly virtually unopposed, and Hamas would be excluded from Palestinian decision-making. But if it rejected violence, a condition of taking part, its own militant followers might accuse the leadership of betrayal and of effectively acceding to the Israel-PLO agreement. The pro-boycott radicals prevailed and Hamas abstained from the January 1996 elections. Monitored by international observers, the elections saw Arafat win 88 per cent of the vote in a turnout which ranged from 85 per cent in Hamas' Gaza stronghold to 30 per cent in Hebron, where the heavy Israeli security presence inhibited Palestinian voters. Both Arafat's authority and his political legitimacy were confirmed. Hamas radicals and their opponents in the leadership, who favoured an accommodation with Arafat's Palestine Authority (PA), had lost their bargaining power.

Hamas' suicide attacks on Israeli buses, avowedly to mark the anniversary of the Hebron massacre and in retaliation for the Israelis' killing of its leading bomb maker, Yahya Ayyash, 'the Engineer', only strained relations with Arafat and the PA further. Hamas aimed to provoke the Israeli public into rejecting the peace process with Arafat. Encouraged by the assassination of Yitzhak Rabin (the one man trusted by the Israeli populace to negotiate a dangerous peace), Hamas hoped to secure the defeat of his successor, Shimon Peres, in the forthcoming Israeli elections by the right-wing Likud opposition. Likud's attitude to the peace process is at best sceptical. With the apparent failure to attain this objective, the announcement by some Hamas elements on 3 March 1996 that the bombing campaign was over may have been intended to mend fences with the PA, but it is doubtful whether the statement represented all the Hamas leadership, while the Dizengoff Street bombing the following day, although widely attributed to PIJ, could only embarrass Arafat. Hamas' ambivalence also extends to hints of violence beyond the Middle East: in August 1995 it warned the US that the extradition to Israel of a senior Hamas official detained there would have 'extremely negative consequences', but earlier it had said it would not harm Western interests.

Politically, the radicals' position, even within Hamas, is less strong than in may sometimes appear. Hamas' popular support has been damaged by Israel's closure of its borders after each act of terrorism. Gaza is especially hard hit, since its economy depends on the thousands of Gazans who cross the border daily to work in Israel. Economic hardship lessens the cost to Arafat in popular sympathy when he responds to Israeli demands that his security forces act against Hamas. Despite the attacks, the Israeli Labour Government coalition and the PLO were committed to work together for peace, with the US and the international community, whose economic investment is huge, while the peace process has gone too far for a future Likud Government simply to reject it. Nor can Hamas look to neighbouring Arab states for support. Egypt and Jordan have peace treaties with Israel and the Jordanian branch of Hamas seems to see its future as a political party in Jordan's emerging democracy. Syria is a lukewarm participant in the peace process, but no Arab state has matched Syria in the savagery of its suppression of Hamas' parent organisation, the Muslim Brotherhood. Lebanon will follow Syria's political lead. While the potential effect of suicide bombers on Israeli opinion can never be discounted, Hamas may find that, having rejected a pragmatic accommodation with Arafat, it will then fail to break the peace process by violence. If so, most members will probably merge back into the Muslim Brotherhood, to pursue their objectives by political means, while the violent diehards could join PIJ.

On the Jewish side, despite the assassination of Rabin and death threats to Peres, the defeat of the religious extremists appeared more predictable. The process of handing over the territories occupied in 1967 to the Palestinians was in progress, the settlers' desperation notwithstanding. Most settlers were tempted to the Occupied Territories by economic inducements and could, if the political will exists, be tempted back into Israel by more of the same. Orthodox believers, living at holy sites, may opt to live under a Palestinian administration. The extremists have been outflanked by the peace process and the unprecedented convergence of Israeli and Palestinian aims. All except the extremists on both sides have an interest in a solution based on partition of the land, at least partly fulfilling the ambitions of the majority. There is no certainty of success but, as the former Israeli Foreign Minister, Abba Eban, observed, people behave sensibly when all other options are exhausted.

Islam in Government and in Opposition
Iran

In the West, perceptions of Islam as the enemy after Communism have made objective consideration of Iran difficult. Iran is seen as destabilising and a threat until proved otherwise. Yet, since the revolution, the government's problem has been to find ways of governing a difficult society. It cannot move too far towards either pragmatism or 'fundamentalist', and Shi'ite, Islam, but under Rafsanjani is moving towards 'Islamic pragmatism', which means raising tolerance levels.

Khomeini's revolution was the triumph of idealism over realism, but realism soon reasserted itself. The intended new Islamic identity was not achieved. The ideology called for wider economic benefits and so won over the lower, middle and bazaari merchant classes to the side of the 'ulema (the clergy). The 'ulema united various disparate groups, but thereby created a mini-state of particular interests and centres of power, ensconced in the Shi'ite hierarchies which formed part of the state structure. These groups' economic interests frequently obstructed government policies, while Khomeini played them off against each other, to maintain a balance.

The Iraqi invasion of 1980 united the factions, but increased the powers of the mini-state. Iran could have ended the war in a position of strength, but its wish to punish Iraq led to six more unnecessary years of bloodshed. Ambitions to extend Iranian hegemony were thwarted when the US forced an end to the fighting. Khomeini's ambitions blinded him to the fact that the two superpowers would never allow him to win and that Iran simply lacked the power to change the political landscape. However, the stalemate helped prepare the ground for a move towards pragmatism and away from revolutionary romanticism. Islamic principles could not be compromised, but pragmatism, accepting the world as it is, and compromise, in order to make social progress, have been largely forced on Iran by events.

When Khomeini died, he left Iran's economy devastated, its image tarnished and the country exhausted by war. The government had to deliver benefits and assert itself, or risk being overthrown. Rafsanjani aimed to curb the mini-state and undo Khomeini's bureaucratic structure. In his foreign policy, he has tried to be both pragmatist and Islamic, a policy tested by Iraq's invasion of Kuwait, which brought US troops to the Gulf, something even the Shah had opposed. Iranian hardliners wanted to side with Iraq, as an Islamic country, and because they feared a permanent US presence. Rafsanjani knew that Iran was too exhausted and the US too strong. He prevailed and Iran benefited, improving its image generally and its relations with the member states of the Gulf Co-operation Council in particular. Saddam was pushed back to the 1975 lines. Iran's rival was defeated: ironically, the US had done for Iran what Khomeini had failed to do.

Further evidence for Iranian pragmatism includes its stance on the conflict between Christian Armenia and Muslim Azerbaijan, where national interest rather than Islamic solidarity dictates policy. But on the negative side are the Rushdie case and Iran's support for the enemies of the Arab-Israel peace process. Iran's support for Hizbullah, especially in view of its Lebanon-based rocket attacks on Israel in April 1996, sits ill with its statements that, if the Palestinians and Syrians want peace with Israel, Iran will not object. Yet it would be a mistake to discount the positive. An Iranian Islamic Republic is here to stay and will remain at heart a revolutionary state much influenced by the mini-state within. There is no obvious response, but the West should recognise Iran's pragmatic tendencies and try to strengthen them.

Algeria

Algeria's recent violent history has encompassed both stalemate and anarchy. Islamists want to replace an impure state with an Islamic state, but most Algerians, including the army, oppose this. So do neighbouring states and France. Secularists want a French-style republic, but this too is rejected by most Algerians. Different and conflicting solutions are now suggested. Firstly, compromise within a pluralist constitutional framework. This is distrusted both by the army and by the neighbours, Morocco and Tunisia, apprehensive at the prospect of democratic participation by Islamic 'fundamentalists'. Secondly, a militarist compromise or 'Sudanese solution', imposed from Algiers; but this would produce ethnic minority resistance in Kabylia, probably comparable to the resistance of the southern Sudanese. Also opposed by France, a 'Sudanese solution' appears no solution at all.

The Algerian stalemate dates from 1992, when the army forced out President Chadhli. The regime has been powerful enough to thwart, but not to defeat, the Islamist opposition. The Presidency lacks a constitutional framework: Zeroual may now be able to provide the leadership to confront the continuing crisis or he may prove only to have rejigged the stalemate. Anarchy has prevailed, so that now the central question is how should Algeria be governed, not who should hold power. Already there are secessionist tendencies in Sahara province while Kabylia, a centre of Berber secularists, could opt for isolation as a 'safe haven' from the violence of the Islamic 'fundamentalists'. Without a remedy, there could be a Polish-style partition. This is the worst case, but the survival of the Algerian state is in question.

Violence originated from the attempt to dissolve the Islamic Salvation Front (French initials, FIS) in early 1992. FIS had been legalised in 1989 when Chadhli had sought to make the Islamists his allies against his internal critics. However, FIS was banned after it had won the elections. Outlawing the FIS made rebellion inevitable and provided an opportunity for the violent groups such as the Islamic Salvation Army (French initials, AIS) and the Armed Islamic Groups (French initials, GIA), which latter has vowed to eradicate all 'Jews, Christians and polytheists' in Algeria, to thrive. These events stemmed from changes in the regime in the 1980s, when religious elements exploited Islamist sentiment, exacerbated by economic failures, to achieve effective autonomy. Previously, the Algerian governments of the 1960s and 1970s had carefully 'managed' religion. As far back as 1955, seven years before it assumed power, the National Liberation Front (French initials, FLN) had recognised that Islam must be the official religion.

Tentative efforts are being made to achieve a solution. In October 1994 Zeroual proposed reducing his three year presidential term by a year, in order to accommodate presidential elections in 1995. Then, the FLN and FIS met in Rome and negotiated a 'National Contract'. In theory not opposed to Zeroual's proposal, in practice it was difficult to reconcile, since the 'National Contract' presupposed an end to violence by accommodating Islamists and re-legalising FIS. But FIS was also required to accept the National Contract's call for pluralism and to abandon its 'theological' ambitions. FIS accepted the National Contract, largely because its ambition for an Islamic state has always been less than serious. However the regime rejected it and proceeded with its own plans.

Hence the National Contract parties boycotted the Presidential elections, thereby mistakenly losing an opportunity to move towards legitimacy and constitutionality. The elections, held in November 1995, were reckoned to be generally free and fair. An effective security operation attracted a 75 per cent turnout, in which Zeroual took 60 per cent of the vote. Moderate Islamists took 25 per cent. Some observers saw this a a setback for FIS, while others thought FIS votes had gone to the moderate Islamists. The elections were well received in the West. Zeroual's position as President has been legitimised, but he is still constrained by dependence on the army, while all the major problems remain. There has been no progress on legitimising FIS, no end to violence (in which the AIS is now widely seen as the military wing of FIS) and no amelioration of economic problems, such as unemployment and the cost of living. While the projected legislative elections may provide an opportunity for progress, Algeria's prospects for a return to constitutional government by political rather than coercive means remain in doubt.

How should the West respond to Iran, Algeria, and the wider Islamic world? The threats and dangers are real – France is necessarily concerned over the dangers of any 'spillover' from Algeria to its four million Muslims residents, but exaggeration and self-fulfilling prophecies must be avoided. The West sees democracy, secularism and pluralism as necessary contemporary virtues; human rights, interdependence and geographical intermingling as the norms for today's world. It sees Islamists as undemocratic, although the West has shown few scruples over the democratic credentials of its own past and present clients in the Islamic world. Many Muslims see the West's democracy as contributing to the social problems which they wish to exclude from their own societies. Western attempts to export ideas are often counter-productive. For example, French encouragement of Berber secularism in Algeria merely divided the would-be democrats. Outsiders may best help by leaving states and societies to work out their own solutions. For example, in Iran a concept of 'guardianship' is developing, which at least implies reciprocal responsibilities between rulers and ruled.

Conventional wisdom calls for the West to make as much effort to understand Islam as it did to understand Communism. Proponents of greater understanding cite powerful strategic, security, economic and political arguments to support their case. But does it really matter what 'fundamentalists' in Iran and Algeria do? Ultimately, they need the world more than it needs them. If they become 'unmanageable' they can be ignored. The FIS is concerned only with Algeria: there is no 'Islamic International'; only the Muslim Brotherhood wants to spread around the Islamic world. Even if there were Islamic governments, they would still be divided by cultural, ethnic and other differences.

4 Case Studies: Asia

Pakistan: Can a Muslim Society Function in a Secular State?

Pakistan, at its inception in 1947, was secular and tolerant of non-Muslims, despite being created as the sub-continent's Muslim homeland. But hopes that it might become a role model for tolerance have been disappointed: Hindus have left, while Christians and non-conforming Muslims are persecuted, although not by the government. In its early days, Pakistan was nationalist, under the influence of immigrants from India, whose demands were secular, not religious. Under Mohammed Ali Jinnah and his successors, Islam had a small role.

A major agent of the change in Pakistan was Maulana Maududi (1903-1979), founder of the Jami'at al-Islami (Islamic Association). A journalist and Islamic thinker, Maududi believed that Islam must be dominant in any nominally Muslim country.

Initially, he opposed the creation of Pakistan, believing the whole sub-continent should be Muslim. During the 1960s and under the premiership of Zulfiqar Ali Bhutto, Maududi's ideas exerted considerable influence. Bhutto, a populist politician who failed to deliver, led a government which was really appointed by the generals: hence the government's quest for popularity was also one for legitimacy. To gain support, Bhutto appeased the religious right, making concessions to the Mullahs which included moving the day of rest from Sunday to Friday and banning alcohol. Most significantly, Zulfiqar Bhutto 'de-Islamised' the Ahmadi sect, something which Maududi had specifically demanded. The Ahmadiyya were better educated and held important posts in the foreign office, the air force and broadcasting. Their down-grading opened up jobs for others and opportunities to exert political patronage. In recent years, however, the position of the Ahmadiyya has improved.

General Zia al-Haq, who overthrew Zulfiqar Bhutto, outmanoeuvred the politicians and introduced limited democracy. But he also advanced Islamic influence – despite Islamist accusations that he did too little, establishing Sharia courts in parallel with the English common law courts inherited from the colonial era. The dominant and deciding area, the Punjab power-base of the military, did not then have religious problems *per se*, despite its large Shia minority. But conflicts have since grown, largely because of propaganda generated by religious parties funded by the Saudis since the 1960s. The Sunni-Shi'ite conflict in Punjab, exacerbated by the long Iran-Iraq war, is close to civil war. Extremism has spread from small towns and rural areas to big cities and the capital. Activist organisations have proliferated, often connected with religious colleges which are forcing grounds for intolerant fanatics bent on persecuting the Shia.

While religion is a factor for political instability in itself, it can reinforce other causes of instability. These are as diverse as the population explosion and the narcotics trade, but the greatest threat is that of ethnic violence between the diverse and often tribal elements of Pakistani society – which Islam does little to unite. The breakdown of order in Karachi is not rooted in religion, but in intercommunal rivalries, particularly those involving the Muhajirs, originally Muslim immigrants from India in 1947. The 'Islamic' label is used by virtually every political group and is frequently linked to nationalist appeals, including by the army. Such exploitation for sectional interests largely precludes its use as a rallying-cry for unity. The army itself, one of Asia's most efficient, is now affected by Islamic influences among younger officers, but seems to have no ambitions to take political power because it is confident in its influence on the government.

With all its problems, Pakistan has an elected, woman-led government in power. The religious groups do not control the government, but have the ability to instigate a spiral of violence. Hence Islamic parties such as the Jami'at Islami, despite their electoral failures, wield power and are able to articulate the grievances of a wider public.

Hindu Nationalism: Setting the Political Agenda?

The destruction of the Ayodhya Mosque in December 1992 brought home to the wider world the strength of Hindu nationalist feeling at the popular level. Politically, nationalist sentiments find expression particularly in the Bharatiya Janata Party (BJP), whose success in the 1996 elections was followed by its inability to form a government. The party has already obliged other political parties to incorporate some of its themes into their own programmes. These, advocated by the BJP and allied parties, can be summed up in the concept of 'Hindutva' or 'Hinduness', which is not a narrowly religious concept but is easily assimilated to a cultural definition of nationalism and citizenship enjoying a wide appeal beyond the ranks of the BJP.

Indian 'fundamentalist' preachers such as those of the Arya Samaj, the most important religious movement in North India in the 20th century, sought to consolidate the Hindu community on the basis of a literal reading of the Vedas, the Hindu's most sacred scriptures, and to re-convert those who had embraced Islam or Christianity. Its purification rituals were a major source of Hindu-

Muslim conflict. Gandhi widened the nationalist appeal by invoking a religious but not necessarily Hindu course of action which spoke to people at the local level. Gandhi realised he must mobilise rural opinion to undermine the raj. However, he was widely interpreted in Hindu terms: his non-violence and fasting were very much in the Hindu tradition. Despite some overtures to the Muslims, he remained at best an ambivalent figure to the Muslim community.

At independence in 1947, Indian nationalism was caught between territory, culture and shared values. On the one hand Nehru saw India as a composite culture (Hindu, Muslim, Buddhist, even Western) historically merging into an harmonious whole. On the other, V.D. Savarkar, long imprisoned by the British for his militancy, held that the only true Indian was one who acknowledged India to be his or her holy land. The creed was unimportant. After independence, Nehru's secularism dominated India, with the emphasis on such themes as economic planning, social development and international non-alignment. Even protests from India's first president, Rajendra Prasad, against the 'modernisation' of Hindu marriage and inheritance laws, were swept aside.

Nehru's ideas survived his death in 1964, but under Mrs Gandhi the position changed slightly as she began to explore the electoral value of a visible Hindu tilt. But it was only after her assassination in October 1984 that a major shift in the political agenda becomes apparent. Realising the importance of politics as a means of self-affirmation and national assertion, the BJP began to make major gains. It also broadened its caste appeal, downwards, in contrast to the Congress Party with its reserved offices and patronage. In 1985 and 1986, arguments over Muslim personal law pointed to a general discontent with what some saw as pandering to minority interests. Then the campaign to demolish the Ayodhya mosque became the focus of discontent and agitation across India. The BJP, exploiting its increased appeal, pushed Prime Minister Narasimha Rao in a Hindu direction during his premiership. Although Rao promised to rebuild the mosque, he did nothing for fear of public reaction.

A factor in the changed agenda has been the exhaustion by the late 1960s of the Congress Party's traditional methods, which effectively exchanged votes for the distribution of resources. Mrs Gandhi tried to substitute her own charisma, but this too faded by the late 1970s. The post-independence middle class now sought something beyond the Congress politics of interests and votes. The BJP has moved to fill the gap. It exploits the discontents arising from rapid economic change, making foreigners the scapegoats. Its recently-launched 'swadeshi' campaign of economic nationalism, emphasising indigenous production and self-reliance, led in August 1995 to the cancellation of the Enron power station deal, the largest ever foreign investment in India. At a lesser level, the BJP campaigns ardently against emblems of American culture such as Kentucky Fried Chicken restaurants.

If the BJP had become the dominant partner in a coalition government in 1996, it would probably have come to a *modus vivendi* with the Muslim minority, which would be tolerated if it accepted an inferior position. On the question of whether Muslims should have their own law, the BJP can stand on the Constitution, which says that India should have one law. This would have pleased the majority while offending the Muslim minority, but the political advantages of pleasing the former outweigh the disadvantages of offending the latter. The BJP would have demanded a more open economy and more investment in education. Its campaigns against Coca Cola and Kentucky Fried Chicken notwithstanding, it can accommodate small and large business interests (the Enron deal has been re-negotiated) and, in international financial matters, like other Indian parties, well knows that World Bank and other international institutional investment in India is so vast that the creditors would not dare foreclose.

In government, it is likely that the BJP would have conformed to the norms of Indian politics rather than attempt seriously to transcend them. In October 1995, the BJP government in the state of Gujarat almost collapsed as a result of personal rivalries. Although the BJP's strength is its national appeal, here too there are clear rivalries between the present party leader, L.K. Advani, and several of his colleagues. Congress and other political parties exploited these difficulties. However, the current problems are resolved; the BJP, whatever its radical intentions, may find itself kept within Indian political conventions, thus following the traditions of Hindu nationalism since the 19th century.

Islam in South-East Asia

Although the the largest Muslim region in terms of population, South-East Asia is notably lacking in religious extremism. The region's 200 million Muslims, 'the silent majority of Islam', contribute the largest numbers of annual pilgrims to Mecca. All south-east Asian states with large Muslim populations, mainly Malaysia, Indonesia, Singapore and the Philippines, are basically secular and have been so from pre-colonial days. In Brunei, Islam was used to reinforce the Sultan's position and other rulers also added Islam to their credentials. The colonial powers reinforced the separation of church and state, a practice maintained by the successor states after independence. There is no prospect that that Indonesia and Malaysia will become Islamic states, but the late 20th century has witnessed some hardening of attitudes between those who want strict observance of Islamic tenets and those who want a more liberal social order. Compromise is now more difficult.

Indonesian Muslims are 'hopelessly' divided among themselves. Between 1962 and 1965, when Communist pressures were strongest, Muslims made some semblance of a united front. But this unity did not last after the communist threat was removed. It is an Indonesian irony that the Modernists are more 'fundamentalist' than the traditionalists. It is the former who want to return to literal Qur'anic texts; the traditionalists are more flexible. They are little concerned by who is in government, so long as they are free pursue their own religious lives. The government was quick to ban Salman Rushdie's *Satanic Verses,* but the traditionalists dismissed the Iranian fatwa as a Shi'ite excess, feeling that Rushdie's punishment was best left to God. Indonesian Islam is generally tolerant of other religions: some 10 per cent of Indonesians are Christian.

The Indonesian government has sought to ensure that religion remains compatible with politics. In accordance with Indonesia's national motto, 'Unity in Diversity', the 'Pancasila' idea tried to contain different religious and political groups within one body, to underpin government philosophy. This caused some dissension, despite assurances that acceptance of 'Pancasila' did not mean putting God second. The government has also taken practical measures. To improve instruction at the Islamic University and at Islamic schools, it is sending 300 Muslim lecturers to be trained abroad to Ph.D and Masters' levels, but deliberately not to the Middle East. Indonesian citizens making the pilgrimage to Mecca are also required to obtain special passports, perhaps also indicative of Indonesian misgivings on the Middle East. Historically, Middle Eastern conflicts have had echoes in South-East Asia: Wahhabism led to war in Sumatra, and one party invited Dutch intervention to resist it. Not all Middle Eastern influences have been destructive: the Islamic thinkers and reformers Mohammed Abduh and Jamal ad-Din al-Afghani had considerable influence on South-East Asian reform movements.

Relations between Indonesian Muslims and their government are cooperative. The main Indonesian religious body actually stopped the Indonesian Constitution from being religiously-orientated. Indonesia has also suggested the establishment of a new Islamic law school, a proposal which must carry weight, coming from the world's largest Muslim country. If successful, this would be a major development in world Islam: the four main traditional law schools are Middle Eastern in origin. *Prima facie,* the suggestion seems a further indication of Indonesian dissatisfaction with Middle Eastern and traditional Islamic influences.

Malaysia is more committed to links with the Islamic world and, unlike Indonesia, uses Islam to assert a Malay character. Malaysia's attitude to 'Asian values' which stress the well-being of the community rather than the individual, is also affected by ethnicity. Associated with the Singapore Chinese leader, Lee Kuan Yew, 'Asian values' have been echoed by Dr Mahathir; their emphasis on the work ethic and rejection of Western criticism on human rights have attracted considerable attraction. But while Dr Mahathir is critical of the West which he portrays as 'degenerate', having rejected spiritual faith and communal life, he has also criticised unspecified Muslim societies for their lack of humanitarianism and democracy. For him, 'Asian values' have a spiritual dimension and Malaysia is careful to emphasise that they do not replace religious values, Islamic or otherwise. Malaysia's successful economy can be seen as an expression of 'Asian values' in practice and, like other booming South-East Asian economies, a barrier to political or religious extremism.

Could Islamism Provoke Destabilisation in Central Asia?

Islam reached southern Central Asia in the eighth century, spreading more slowly into the north. The Soviet period brought major change. An uneasy initial accommodation between Islam and the Communist government was followed by a harder government attitude by the end of the 1920s. Religion and the state were separated, the Sharia replaced, the Western calendar imposed and women unveiled. The scale and the speed of change were unknown elsewhere: the untrammelled totalitarian state used coercion and terror freely. In Kazakhstan in the 1930s, half the population was wiped out, not simply by religious persecution, but by the collectivisation of agriculture and the settlement of the nomads.

By the 1940s and 1950s, a whole generation of Central Asians had been cut off from their traditional way of life. The institutional structure of Islam had been destroyed. Parents were afraid even to talk to their children about religious matters. Some customs survived, such as visits to the tombs of holy men and some practices, such as burials. So thorough was the Soviet repression that by the 1950s, it was difficult to find a Central Asian able to recite the *shehadeh*, the Muslim profession of faith. Only a few mystics (Sufis) reputedly maintained some vaguely-remembered rituals. For reasons of foreign policy, particularly to reassure and befriend Islamic countries, the Soviet government established showpiece mosques, libraries and other Islamic institutions.

The 1980s witnessed a religious resurgence throughout the Soviet Union, including of Islam in Central Asia and there were perhaps some 8,000-10,000 believers in Central Asia by the end of the decade. But the real Islamic revival came with the collapse of the Soviet Union. Not only the people, but the Central Asian leadership turned to Islam en masse as a source of legitimisation. Leaders who had come up through the Soviet system re-emerged overnight as Muslims. These new/old leaders now took oaths of office on the Qur'an, but were careful to retain control: they intended Islam to bolster their leadership, not to destabilise it. A second facet of the revival was that of Islamic culture, with renewed interest in Islamic architecture, codes of behaviour, social norms and other aspects of Islamic life. While attendances at mosques soon declined, a cultural identity was successfully created. A third manifestation of the revival involved the young and urban. Disillusioned with the Soviet Union, they soon became disillusioned with the West and sought instead an 'orthodox', rigorous Islam. Some critics feared that they wanted to alter society again, for example, by reversing the emancipation of women.

The Islamic revival in Central Asia thus had three strands: state-sponsored, cultural and religious. It is too soon to predict how these will develop, but there are four possibilities for the future. First, Islam could be used by any or all of the new states' leaderships if they felt threatened, either internally by economic failure or externally by threats to state borders. Islam could be used to mobilise opinion against such threats. Perhaps ominously, the Muslim leaders most admired in Central Asia are Saddam and Qadhafi. Second, as the new states are authoritarian and suppress debate, opposition groups may try to rally support under an Islamic banner. Third, as in Tajikistan, particular clans or tribes may adopt Islam as a quasi-political platform. Fourth, there might be a spontaneous and genuine mass Islamic religious revival throughout the region, although this is unlikely.

Of all threats to the stability of the Central Asian states, that of growing economic inequality is the greatest. Under the Soviet system, the Communist 'nomenklatura' enjoyed great privileges, but they were discreet and the system was 'democratic' in that the lowest could climb up the Communist Party hierarchy, from remote village to the Kremlin. Now, an urban elite has been created which creams off the benefits, creating a conspicuous nouveau riche class. In contrast, ordinary people, the old middle class and the peasants are getting poorer, with no hope of joining the boom. In some areas, barter has reappeared. Those excluded from the new prosperity are alienated and beginning to consider that their plight resulted from a Western conspiracy to 'keep them down'. Economic woes are exacerbated by emigration, as the more able leave to find better opportunities for their children. Kazakhstan and Uzbekistan are trying hard to stem this exodus.

Nation-building following the collapse of the Soviet Union is a major problem. The southern republics were Soviet creations, their 'national myths' largely created by the Communists on ideological grounds, designed to show tribal structures developing to become part of the Soviet nation. The myth now has to be re-crafted, taking out the Soviet elements. The choice may be between an aggressive nationalism or Islam, or maybe a combination of the two, as in Kazakhstan. The Soviet authorities had associated Islam with backwardness and such practices as child marriages. But it had also encouraged local languages and thriving local libraries, which contributed greatly to nation-building. Although the intellectuals had had little idea of Islam, some cultural influences had survived and Islam may now become a vehicle for cultural identity and local languages. However, this carries its own dangers, as language differences could be a destabilising influence in multi-ethnic republics. Despite the history of Soviet oppression, Central Asians had pride in being Soviet citizens and thus members of a super-power. They now tend to look for an authoritarian, father figure and an established way of life, which not only echoes the Soviet system but also the pre-Soviet khans.

The influence of other Islamic and Middle Eastern countries on Central Asia is limited. Central Asians now realise that Turkey is not a member of the EU, has its own economic problems, and is generally less educated than they are. Its businessmen are appreciated, as are its scholarships, but Central Asians, the former citizens of a super-power, resent Turkish condescension. Turkey also lacks direct communication with Central Asia, while its Western connections are a liability. Iran is cautious: there is an Islamic division between Sunni Central Asia and Shi'ite Iran, while Tehran realises that there is no established Muslim culture on which to build. Turkmenistan, with its oil and transport links, is of most concern to Iran. Missionaries from Egypt, Pakistan and elsewhere have crowded in to remedy the lack, as they see it, of Islamic scholarship in the *madrassehs* (religious schools), where works on Islam are largely in Russian and English. In Uzbekistan, Saudi missionaries are resented for their high-handedness. Economically, Central Asians now look further afield than the Middle East and here their outlook is secular. They are attracted by successful economic models – China, Japan, South-East Asia, even Australia. In particular, they see themselves as a future source of raw materials for Japan, even an alternative oil source to the Middle East.

The West is in an unfortunate position: politically, it is regarded with suspicion and sometimes blamed, however unjustly, for economic privations. Its aid has led to corruption, since there is no effective government machinery to handle it. Aid should aim to by-pass governments, going directly to small-scale projects, such as English-language teaching. While so many uncertainties persist, it will be impossible for the West to formulate an adequate response.

5 Case Studies: Europe

Former Yugoslavia: The Role of Religion in the Creation of National Identities and in Promoting War

The conflict in the former Yugoslavia is not primarily religious. Although non-observance is widespread, there has been a revival in both Catholic and Serb Churches, as well as in Mosques. Religious observance often marks an assertion of nationality. The Churches, weakened under Communism, have seen an opportunity in war to regain influence and property.

The former Yugoslavia is historically a land of conflict and division: in the fourth century it was split in three by the Emperor Theodosius, an action which was to influence the development of national identity centuries later. The Ottomans, reputedly intolerant of other religions, in fact accorded considerable freedom to non-Muslim communities under the 'millet' administrative system, which gave the Orthodox Church considerable autonomy. The 'millet' system effectively became the cradle for the later nations, but the Catholics were not granted an autonomous 'millet', owing to Rome's alliance with the Ottomans' enemies. In 1557, the Ottomans restored the Pecs Orthodox Patriarchate, retrospectively a significant step in the association of nationality and religion. By the later nineteenth century, Greece, Serbia and Montenegro possessed national Orthodox churches which laid much emphasis on national rituals. Conscious of the freedom they enjoyed under the Turks, many Serb Christians fought for the Ottoman Empire in its wars against the Catholic powers of Western Europe.

Croatia and Slovenia were Catholic. While the Slovene Church remained loyal to the Habsburgs, Croatia's concern was to recapture ground lost to the Orthodox Serbs, simultaneously restoring Catholic influence. After the First World War, the Catholic bishops professed support for the broader Yugoslav state. Although their real aim was to expand Catholic influence, commitment to a broader concept at least meant less attachment to links between the Church and the existing, smaller states which would be subsumed in the new Yugoslavia. In all these developments, Islam played no unifying role for the Muslim peoples. There were no links between the Kosovo Albanians and the Bosnian Muslims and no Islamic arc drawing together Muslims in Greece, Serbia and Bulgaria.

The current conflict is rooted in the first Yugoslavia, which lasted from 1918 to 1941. The Slovenes and Croats assumed that the communities would be equal, but the Serbs sought a Greater Serbia. The Serbian Orthodox Church, although lacking the intellectual rigour and Holy Orders which distinguished the Catholics, became an instrument of 'Serbianisation'. The Second World War witnessed a series of conflicts in which the churches played political roles. In Croatia, the Catholic Church opposed the Communist-led partisans who fought the Nazis and their proteges. Hence between 1941 and 1945 the Church did not distance itself from the regime. On the Serb side, the Serbian Orthodox Church did not reject links with the Chetniks. The Muslims endeavoured simply to survive amid competing Serb and Croat claims.

Under the Communist regime of Marshal Tito, the Muslims were given some autonomy in various areas as Yugoslavs, although the Communists intended that they should have a cultural, not a religious, Islamic identity. The three groups lived together, as Bosnians first and Serbs, Croats or Muslims second. All were secularised, the Serbs most, the Croats least, with the Muslims, who in 1968 were embarrassed to be classified as such, in between. The Serbian Church never criticised Communist power, as the Catholics did.

The outbreak of hostilities in 1992 marked the growth of ambitions – especially Serb, for a Greater Serbia. Tito had in effect dismembered Serbia. Old historical claims were revived and the Church saw its opportunity to regain lost influence. The Muslims were considered renegades, and as Arab inferiors left over from the Ottomans. It fell to the Orthodox Church the task of de-legitimising the Muslims, in preparation for ethnic cleansing. The Church 'demonised' the Muslims, as the Serbs sought to portray their opponents as genocidal. The Muslims were now obliged to act for their own survival. Their most controversial external assistance came from Iran. The Catholic Church has been less involved, although the bishops supported the Croat reconquest of lost territory. The hierarchy has been under considerable grassroots pressure, but the Church has distanced itself from some of President Tudjman's activities, condemned some atrocities and has appealed to Serbs to return to their homes.

Roman Catholicism in Poland

Although Poland embraced Catholicism more than 1,000 years ago, it was in the recent past a multi-ethnic, multi-faith state, with Protestants and Jews also well represented. Between the two world wars, Catholics amounted to some 45 per cent of the population but after the Second World War they accounted for 95 per cent. During the 45 years of Communist rule which followed World War Two, the Church became a political actor. The Communists stripped it of wealth and privilege, but the Church was too strong for them to destroy. The resolute stand of Cardinal Wyshinsky in 1953 secured for the Church an autonomy unique under Comunist rule. Poland was then still largely a peasant country, and the Church was particularly strong in rural areas. The Communists were wary of provoking the peasants over agricultural collectivisation. In time the Church became, if not overtly, a magnet for opponents of the regime. In the 1970s and 1980s, the Church supported workers' movements and gained confidence from the 1978 election of a Polish Pope and his subsequent visits to the country.

Since 1989, Poland has been deeply divided over Church issues. When Lech Walesa appointed the first non-Communist government since the Second World War, there were widespread feelings of indebtedness to the Church. The fate of Father Jerzy Popieluszko, the priest and member of Lech Walesa's Solidarity trade union movement, kidnapped, tortured and killed by the

Communists loomed large in the popular memory. Hence pro-Catholic parties, dominated by Solidarity members, entered parliament, but their activities soon helped discredit the Church. Parliament quickly enacted a bill for compulsory religious education and sought to make abortion punishable by two years in jail. Restitution of Church property began in 1989, but inflated claims, going back to Tsarist times and including German Catholic property, caused resentment as Poles questioned why the Church should enjoy such priority. The Church has also received a radio licence and has television facilities, in addition to its press outlets. 'Catholic Action', a pre-Second World War organisation, was revived with Papal approval, seeking to create Catholic cells in workplaces. In the army, Communist political instructors were replaced by priests, while Catholic lay organisations aimed to prevent the separation of Church and state. In the debate over the new Constitution, some bishops accepted a limited role and other political figures were anxious to avoid discrimination against non-Catholics. But extreme Church demands included references in the Constitution to the unborn child and decency in the media.

Resentment against the autocratic attitude of the Church led to the return of many Leftist candidates, some former Communists, in the 1993 general elections. The return of the Left in politics prompted a vigorous Church response, particularly concerning the new Constitution. The conflict between Church and State appeared increasingly to be between the Church and democracy. Some senior clerics said that the Church would never be compatible with democracy, since it is based on unchanging natural law, which cannot be altered by political fashions. Hardliners insisted that abortion was against God's law, hence no change was possible. The Church was also reportedly seeking ways to ban contraception and divorce. Its opponents, backed by widespread popular feeling that the Church wielded too much influence in politics, countered that it is not possible to legislate morality.

With parliamentary support ebbing, the Church clung tenaciously to its 1989 gains. But its traditional role had derived from

Poland's lack of opportunity to develop into a modern state. During 45 years of Communism, the Church had been in an unnatural position. Like its ally, Solidarity, the Church found it easier to maintain support when opposing Communism than under a democratic political system. Opposition had enabled the Church to harness the stubborn, resistant Polish character to its purpose. Under Communism, Poles could attend Mass and defy the regime. Progress towards becoming a modern nation, based on democratic stability, seemed inevitably to be at the expense of Church authority. In the Presidential elections of November 1995, when President Walesa was defeated by the former Communist Party official, Alexander Kwasniewski, Walesa's supporters proved to be the older, poorer Poles; Kwasniewski's the younger and more forward-looking. Although priests are legally barred from political activity, the Polish Episcopate made its pro-Walesa sympathies clear. Walesa shared platforms with clerics. Walesa's defeat is thus also that of the Church.

In the future, the Church seems destined for a less political role and a period of reform. Cut off by Communism from the influence of Vatican II, Polish Catholicism is far more bureacratic and authoritarian than its Western liberal counterpart. Its cherished role, as a bastion of the West against Eastern influences, the Orthodox Churches as well as Communism, is being overtaken as European barriers come down. The Polish Church sees a re-Christianising mission for itself in Europe, but may first have to face painful readjustment at home.

6 The Forgotten Fundamentalists: Christians in Africa and Latin America

Christian Fundamentalism in Southern Africa

'Fundamentalism' is a particularly unhelpful term in considering African Churches. Their 'very slight sense of past' excludes the historical perspectives found elsewhere in the world. The Dutch

Reformed Church, representing Afrikaner conservative nationalist Protestantism, was the nearest approximation to 'fundamentalism'. For 40 years, it provided Afrikaners with a rationale for apartheid and hegemony. This was stability of a sort, but with a built-in instability, since 75 per cent of the population was excluded. South Africa is now ostensibly less stable, but may prove to have greater long-term stability. Christianity is strong amongst both black and white South Africans. Archbishop Desmond Tutu and others undermined the confidence of (white) Christian bodies in the Afrikaner government's policies. Elsewhere, American 'fundamentalist' groups have supported RENAMO in Mozambique and UNITA in Angola. But while new wave Conservative Evangelicism has backed reactionary white forces in southern Africa, this has been to little political effect. Its chief significance is religious, but often it is apolitical.

Christianity is the 'hegemonic religion' of half of Africa. But the black churches are generally 'other worldly' and have channelled blacks away from political concerns. Despite some clashes with Islam in southern Sudan and Biafra, and extremism on both sides, Christian-Muslim relations have been good, if 'fragile'. Much Middle Eastern money is being spent on mosque building, but many mosques have few adherents. Tanzania, Mozambique and Malawi have large Muslim communities, but there and elsewhere in the southern half of Africa peoples are predominantly of 'traditional' religion or Christian. The number of Muslims is increasing in Zimbabwe, where the original Muslim community dating from the pre-Portuguese coastal trade has been 'rediscovered'. But the number of Christians is growing rapidly in northern Nigeria. Generally, Islam, for which the Arabic Qur'an is the literal Word of God, does not encourage local languages as Christianity does. Islam is not necessarily 'a good religion for Africa': African culture, with its emphasis on dance and music does not always blend easily with Islam, particularly in view of the latter's restrictive attitude towards women. Often, popular Islam and popular Christianity tend to be mixed, while being 'Christian' is a matter of public culture.

The causes of African instability, among them war, poverty, the population explosion, drought, AIDS, corruption and tribal conflict, are not linked to the churches, although the churches are often the only bodies able to grapple with the consequences. Amid the collapse of the institutional networks of governments, universities and trade unions, those of the churches have survived. Church leadership is now almost entirely black (there are 300-400 black bishops), but has retained international, including financial, support. International charities, such as Oxfam, prefer to work through churches, whose leaders are more respected and trusted than governments or political parties. In some countries, bishops are effectively in control, for example Mgr Isidore de Souza, Archbishop of Cotonou, who in 1991-92 oversaw Benin's transition from a single party state towards a multi-party democracy. The influence of Archbishop Tutu in South Africa and, in Uganda, that of the Rt Reverend Mgr Dr John Walligo, secretary of the Constitutional Committee is also apparent. Churches are sources of news, printing presses and other means of communication. They have become 'honest brokers' although churchmen are no more equipped to cope with political and economic problems than lay politicians. In societies whose other institutions are disintegrating, church leaders have been pushed into action, in an attempt to provide stability. Their conspicuous role in the past five years has been unexpected, but they risk being discredited if and when they fail. Tutu is well aware of the dangers of becoming too politicised and forbade Anglican priests to stand for Parliament.

The structure of the churches of southern Africa reflects the political and social changes of recent years. The Dutch Reformed Church has changed its political stance and its membership is now more black than white. The Roman Catholic Church (the largest in Africa, apart from South Africa, where Protestants predominate), Anglican and Methodist Churches are mostly black, but have strong white membership. The churches often take over tribal structures, hence the multiplication of dioceses, so that each can have its own bishop. 'Africanisation' has encouraged denominational separation, as Africans prefer their own denominations. Efforts in the 1950s and 1960s to encourage ecumenism on the lines of the United Church of South India did not succeed. Today there are literally thousands of independent black churches, many very small. Usually impoverished, they sometimes form beneficial links with churches overseas, hence Bishop Muzorewa's links to US Methodists. 'Fundamentalist' evangelical missions from America, such as the Southern Baptists, Asia, South Korea and the Philippines, link up with African churches, although their impact is often superficial. Unlike the missionaries from the older churches, the newcomers are often ignorant of the language and culture.

Rwanda is both the most Christian and the most genocidal country in Africa. Predominantly Catholic, the Hutu originally accepted Christianity more readily than the Tutsi. In the 1930s, the Tutsi realised that they had been left behind politically and they converted to Christianity en masse. Hence, as independence approached in the early 1960s, both the Belgian government and the church missions were worried by Tutsi dominance. Their attempts to redress the balance by support for the Hutu coincided with the social destabilisation of the immediate pre-independence era, leading to the mass exodus of the Tutsi to Uganda between 1959 and 1961. Thereafter, it has been a Hutu ambition to eliminate the remaining Tutsi.

Catholicism, Protestantism and Politics in Latin America

In the past 25 years, evangelical Protestantism has grown threefold in Latin America. Since the mid-1980s, some 15-20 per cent of the populations of Brazil and Chile and up to 30 per cent of Guatemala's have become Pentecostalist. Converts are concentrated among the rising numbers of the poor, hit hardest by the social and economic problems of Latin America. Yet it is impossible to categorise Pentecostal appeal. It is a bigger movement than Liberation Theology and, while it lacks that doctrine's political and social implications, it nonetheless poses a revolutionary challenge to the *status quo* and establishment culture, to 'respectable ways of behaviour'. That *status quo* is in large part the Roman Catholic Church, at whose expense the Pentecostals have mostly made their gains. In some areas, the Catholic Church is described as 'fighting for its life' (only some 15 per cent of Latin American Catholics are active believers). Pentecostals themselves say that, while the Catholics opted for the poor, the poor opted for Pentecostalism.

Pentecostalism is fissile. There are small churches in the favelas (slums), but the overall organisation is run along modern, big business lines, making great use of computers. This 'multinational' approach befits churches which are not confined to Latin America but are a global phenomenon, although the chapels, techniques and approach to the congregation are the same. The leading churches are the 'Assemblies of God' and the 'Universal Church of the Kingdom of God'. The latter, formed some 15 years ago, has two million worshippers in Latin America, Portugal, Angola and the US. It has 2,000 pastors, a television network and radio stations. The churches are run on democratic centralist lines and their leaders have virtually untrammelled power. Pastors, preachers or ministers are rotated from church to church, to prevent them building up a personal following and are well paid. Training for ministers is short: it is a favoured Pentecostal tactic to take individuals such as drug addicts off the streets, reform them, then send them back as ministers in the shortest possible time. Such apparently miraculous transformations impress local communities. There are also numerous stories of former guerriallas exchanging their guns for bibles. The Pentecostals are wealthier than the Roman Catholics, whose wealth is tied up in property. The 'Assemblies of God', whose adherents have membership cards, make checks on members' regular financial contributions. The 'Universal Church' has no membership cards, but also relies on raising money from the local community, rather than from US sympathisers, to fund good works.

For Pentecostals, the defining belief is the gift of the Holy Spirit. Doctrine is largely unimportant. Adult baptism is the sign of the all-important conversion experience. Conversion is linked to healing: a crisis in the convert's life is 'cured' when he or, significantly, she joins the church. The majority of Pentecostal and other evangelical groups are women, often abandoned women, who band together against the depredations of men. Networks of women run social movements, often based on their role of motherhood. The churches give women collective power, which frightens men, often into giving up extra-marital sex and street women. Women claim that they can reconstruct stable families through the churches, where they also meet men better disposed towards them to marry. And men too can find support from the churches, which teach that the real challenge for a man is to remain faithful to one woman.

The Pentecostal churches, with their charismatic interpretation of the Holy Spirit, place less emphasis on Sunday or Easter than conventional churches. While personal activities such as choir-singing are encouraged, there is also pressure to conform, for example, to an austere code of dress. By appealing to popular culture they have attacked the more contrived established norms. Where Liberation Theology aims to take control of society, Pentecostalism urges adherents to take control of themselves.

Politically, Pentecostalism has made its main impact in Guatemala, where there are more than 400 churches. There, Pentecostals were largely responsible for the election of the region's first evangelical President, Jorge Serrano Elias. Money from the US has been important in the Pentecostal success. Peru, Brazil, El Salvador and Honduras may also become evangelical nations, but Pentecostalism seems to have no particular political ideology, simply using politics to advance its own interests. Lack of a formal ideology may be linked to the history of discredited movements of both the Left and the Right in Latin America. Both have led to violence, which the deeply pacific Pentecostals and other Protestants abhor. They reject both revolutionary violence and the organisation of society on military lines.

To its critics Latin American Pentecostalism is a religion of bad taste in architecture, music and dress, the 'fast food' of religion. The Pentecostal church has its shortcomings, notably the lack of training of its ministers in contrast to the Catholic church, whose priests take years to train. The Catholic church is fighting back:

the Pope visited Central America in March 1996, speaking out against the Protestant churches. Pentecostalism may not be a Reformation in the sense of a battle of ideas, but it is re-shaping Latin American society.

7 Conclusions

The examples cited above illustrate the diversity of religious 'fundamentalisms', ranging from the narrow political aims of the would-be saboteurs of the Middle East peace process to the apolitical Pentecostal cultural revolutionaries of Latin America; from the cynical exploitation of religion in the former Yugoslavia to the relaxed attitudes of South-East Asia.

Where religion is associated with political extremism, it usually gets an undeservedly bad press. Religion rarely initiates conflict, hostility and instability, but is exploited for political and particularly nationalist ends. The phenomenon is seen to particularly sombre effect in the former Yugoslavia. When thus exploited, to rally popular support or to be used as an identifying flag or banner, the true essence of religion, the calls for tolerance, respect for differences, for the humanity of others, are quickly forgotten. It is too often judged by the activities of those who distort or betray its message.

How should the West respond to 'fundamentalism'? The question is an oversimplification: more pertinent questions are 'Does the West need to respond?' and 'Is there any response the West can make?' As noted above, there are various types of 'fundamentalism'. Not all are associated with political extremism and not all pose any threat to Western interests. No political response is needed or appropriate to the Pentecostals of Latin America, while the relations between religion and politics in South-East Asia could be copied with advantage elsewhere. Where there is religiously-expressed hostility to the West stemming from issues of identity, speed of social change, cultural factors or the need for reassurance, the scope for a conciliatory response is limited. Peoples must work out their own identities; outsiders will most probably make matters worse. When economic factors exacerbate extremist attitudes, the West may be able to help. Aid is superficially attractive, but it can also be counter-productive, leading to disappointed expectations. It should be well-targeted, and part of a broader package to encourage trade, where the West can help, by opening its markets.

However, it is Islamic 'fundamentalism', particularly in the Middle East, which poses the sharpest problems for the West. And here, while the West may act as a political 'facilitator', encouraging constructive debate, it is the peoples who must tackle the underlying causes. That will mean changing relations between the rulers and the ruled. Arab governments should move towards democracy, the necessary precondition for a vital debate on a separation of religion and politics, essential for regional stability and the creation of institutions capable of bringing general development. Too much power and too many resources remain concentrated in too few hands. It is not enough to say that the answer lies in a return to religion or simpler structures. While the West needs to rediscover its own spirituality to appreciate the importance of religion to Muslims when seeking a dialogue, Muslims must realise that no meaningful dialogue is possible if they insist that theirs is the 'conclusive and only system'. The alternatives are either a reversion to an ugly form of primitive, assertive dogmatic Islamism, or moving towards more participatory politics. Islamic 'fundamentalism' is the successor to failed Arab nationalism and socialism. Short of a reversion to secularism, it is hard to see what could follow, other than instability and chaos.[3]

In his 1996 Easter message, the Pope criticised the instransigence of 'followers of other religions' who persecuted Christians, a thinly-veiled reference to Islamic 'fundamentalists'. The Pope has recently drawn attention to Muslim persecution of Christians in the Sudan, but also calls for Islamic-Christian dialogue. Are

---

[3] These arguments were succinctly made by Sir Allan Ramsey, a British diplomat interviewed on retirement by *The Times* on 4 April 1996.

Muslim 'fundamentalists' prepared for tolerance? Conventional academic wisdom points out that Islam means different things in different places and that the West allows itself to be alarmed into paranoia by the rhetoric of Islamic extremists. Yet in a world where most Islamic states are characterised by lack of democracy, a poor record on human rights, and discrimination against women, but contains a billion Muslims, there is some cause for Western concern. Reassurance is a two-way street.

List of Participants

AHONEN, Risto: The Research Institute; Tampere
AKINER, Shirin: School of African and Oriental Studies, University of London
AMBÜHL, Hansjürg: Federal Department of Foreign Affairs, Berne
BADAWI, Zaki: The Muslim College, London
BLAIR, Donald: United Distillers plc, London
CRAIG, James: Middle East Association, London
CVIIC, Christopher: Royal Institute of International Affairs, London
DAMKJAER, Dorthea: Ministry of Foreign Affairs, Copenhagen
DE MYTTENAERE, Lucie: Ministry of Foreign Affairs, Brussels
DEPPE, Rupert: Thuringia Land Parliament, Erfurt
DUNCAN, Alistair: World of Islam Festival Trust, London
EASTWOOD, Basil: Foreign and Commonwealth Office, London
EL-AWAISI, Abd al-Fattah: University of Stirling, Scotland
FROHOLM, Anne: Ministry of Foreign Affairs, Oslo
FULLER, Martin: Researcher and Writer, Southend-on-Sea
GOLDBERG, David: The Liberal Jewish Synagogue, London
HASTINGS, Adrian: University of Leeds, Leeds
HAUGE, Kåre: Ministry of Foreign Affairs, Oslo
HOLM, Erik: Eleni Nakou Foundation, London
HOTUNG, Ann: Investor, NewYork
HYMAN, Anthony: "Central Asian Survey", London
JOHANSEN, Terje: Norwegian Parliament, Oslo
JONES, Timothy: Foreign and Commonwealth Office, London
JOZIASSE, Barbara: Ministry of Foreign Affairs, The Hague
KRATZ, Ulrich: School of Oriental and African Studies, University of London

LANGHORNE, Richard: Wilton Park, Steyning
LEHMANN, David: University of Cambridge, Cambridge
LITTLE, Jenny: Wilton Park, Steyning
MAYER, Jean-François: Central Office of Defence, Berne
MILANI, Mohsen: St Antony's College, University of Oxford
MORTIMER, Edward: "Financial Times", London
MYERS, Joanne: Carnegie Council on Ethics and International Affairs, New York
ÖRN, Torsten: Embassy of Sweden to The Holy See, Rome
REICHE, Eckhard: Federal German Parliament, Bonn
ROBERTS, Hugh: School of Oriental and African Studies, University of London
SHELLEY, Catherine: Church Action on Poverty, London
STAEL VON HOLSTEIN, Curt: National Swedish Police Board, Stockholm
SWORD, Keith: School of Slavonic and East European Studies, University of London
TAYLOR, David: School of Oriental and African Studies, University of London
THOMSEN, Ulla: Freelance, "Koutoret", Copenhagen
TICKTIN, Miriam: Department of Foreign Affairs and International Trade, Ottawa
TOBLER, Urs: Centre for the Study of Islam and Christian-Muslim Relations, Birmingham
van HASSELT, Willem: Ministry of Foreign Affairs, The Hague
WELP, Dietrich: Federal Ministry of Justice, Bonn
WILCZEK, Marcin: Ministry of Foreign Affairs, Warsaw